Classic
ASIAN

Classic
ASIAN

Tasty traditional recipes from the East

KIM CHUNG LEE

HERMES
HOUSE

This edition published by Hermes House
an imprint of Anness Publishing Limited
Hermes House, 88-89 Blackfriars Road, London SE1 8HA

A CIP catalogue record for this book is available from the British Library

Publisher Joanna Lorenz
Managing Editor Linda Fraser
Designer Val Carless
Illustrator Madeleine David
Jacket Photography Thomas Odulate
Jacket Styling Claire Louise Hunt
Recipes by Kit Chan, Kim Chung Lee, Sarah Gates, Sallie Morris,
Shehzad Husain, Rafi Fernandez and Liz Trigg
Production Controller Joanna King

All recipes and quantities are given in both metric and imperial measures, and, where appropriate, measures are
also given in standard cups and spoons. Follow one set, but not a mixture, because they are not interchangeable.

Printed and bound in Singapore

3 5 7 9 10 8 6 4 2

Picture on frontispiece: Red Chicken Curry with Bamboo Shoots

CONTENTS

INTRODUCTION

Balance is the essence of Asian cooking. From the South China Sea to the Indian Ocean, cooks strive to achieve a harmonious balance of tastes, textures, colours and aromas. Whether a sizzling stir-fry or a mouth-tingling curry, all dishes must be fresh, combining a medley of flavours – hot, sweet, sour, salty or bitter. The diversity of the cuisines of Thailand, India, the Philippines, Pakistan, Indonesia and Vietnam are brought together in this book to provide an introduction to the ingredients, recipes and methods of Asian cooking.

Over the centuries traders and merchants have travelled to Asia in search of valuable spices. The impact of various religions and cultures, such as Buddhism, Christianity and Islam, have left their mark on the cuisines of these countries. The legacy of the invading merchant traders, colonialists and more recently tourists is an expansion in our knowledge and appreciation of the diversity of Asian foods, methods and traditions of cooking.

An Asian meal is an intensely social occasion and will involve many different dishes, which are all placed on the table at the same time and eaten in no particular order. There will always be rice or noodles, soup, curry, a steamed or fried dish, a salad and a dipping sauce or relishes. This buffet-style experience is ideal for Westerners' palates as it encourages experimentation with new ingredients and tastes.

The tropical climates of the vast continent of Asia produce an abundance of fruit, vegetables and flowers. The seas are rich with fish and seafood and the paddy-fields yield excellent rice. By insisting on the best quality ingredients and learning the few simple techniques of Asian cooking described in these recipes, you will be assured of excellent results time after time.

Opposite top to bottom: Soft Fried Noodles and Egg Fried Noodles.

INGREDIENTS

Asian ingredients used to be hard to come by in the West. Recently, however, supermarkets and often health stores have started to stock a huge variety of different herbs, spices, pastes, sauces and condiments, which enable the adventurous cook to tackle even the most exotic dishes from the far-flung corners of the world. If you come across an ingredient you don't recognize in this book, simply go to your nearest supermarket or specialist Asian store and ask – they will probably be more than happy to help.

Herbs and spices play an important part in Asian dishes. Chillies are frequently used, but add them in moderation unless you like your food very hot; green chilli is reputed to be less potent than the fiery red. Jars of chopped chilli are available from supermarkets and are easy to use. *Lengkuas* or *galangal* are other common ingredients. These are members of the ginger family and should be prepared and used in the same way as ginger. They are both available in dried or powdered form, although, as always, fresh is best. Unusual vegetables include *bangkuang*, which looks like a turnip; it should be peeled thinly before use and cut into strips for stir-fries, spring rolls or salads.

Spices and fresh vegetables are the mainstay of Asian cooking.

The sweet, mild taste of many Asian dishes is achieved by adding coconut in one of its many forms. Cream, milk, juice or desiccated, it contributes a delicious texture and taste to many main course and dessert dishes. To counteract the sweetness, sharper tastes such as kaffir lime or lemon grass are used. Kaffir limes are prepared and used as ordinary limes, and can be juiced, chopped or sliced. Lemon grass must be carefully chopped to eliminate the fibrous texture, and is usually removed from the dish before serving. Asian cooks delight in using all parts of a fruit. For example, banana leaves are ingeniously used to line steamers, or to wrap chicken or fish prior to grilling or baking, imparting a light tea-like flavour to the meat. The dark, glossy leaves of the kaffir lime are often added to stews or soups for added zing.

Fish forms a vital part of Asian cuisine. Prawns, squid and crabs are great favourites, and fish sauce is added to many non-fish dishes. It is made from anchovies and has a strong salty flavour. Fish sauce is used in much the same way as soy sauce, for cooking stir-fries, flavouring rice and noodles, or spicing up vegetables. Shrimp paste or *terasi*, which is made from fermented prawns and salt, is also used extensively, and is usually sold in blocks.

Bean curd is another staple of Asian cooking; made from soya bean milk set with gypsum, it is found in the dishes of many countries. It is increasingly popular in the West, especially among vegetarians, who value it as a rich

Woks are the favoured cooking vessel of the Far East, perfect for one-pot dishes. Karahi are similar pans used in Pakistan. Both are ideal for Asian cooking.

source of protein. Bean-sprouts too are packed with vitamins, iron and protein. Sprouted from the mung bean they are used in salads, stir-fries and soups. They should be crisp and firm with little scent. Bean sauce or yellow bean sauce is also popular. It is made from salted, fermented soya beans and is added to flavour all types of savoury dishes.

If at first sight Asian cooking seems to involve a bewildering array of unheard-of ingredients, remember that many of them are cheap to buy and can be stored for a long time if treated properly. Most dried herbs and leaves can be frozen, and many spices keep for months in a cool store cupboard. The use of fresh vegetables and only small amounts of fish and meat means that the cost of preparing Asian dishes should not be high. Traditional dishes are often cooked in a large wok, which feeds many, and the array of small dishes and filling rice or noodle recipes will certainly not leave you feeling hungry.

HANOI BEEF AND NOODLE SOUP

his fragrant North Vietnamese soup, traditionally eaten for breakfast, makes a filling starter.

INGREDIENTS
1 onion
1.5kg/3–3½lb beef shank with bones
2.5cm/1in fresh root ginger
1 star anise
1 bay leaf
2 whole cloves
2.5ml/½ tsp fennel seeds
1 piece of cassia bark or cinnamon stick
3 litres/5 pints/12½ cups water
fish sauce, to taste
juice of 1 lime
150g/5oz fillet steak
450g/1lb fresh flat rice noodles

ACCOMPANIMENTS
1 small red onion, sliced into rings
115g/4oz beansprouts
2 red chillies, seeded and sliced
3 spring onions, finely sliced
handful of coriander leaves
lime wedges

SERVES 4 – 6

1 Cut the onion in half. Grill under a high heat, cut side up, until the exposed sides are caramelized, and deep brown. Set aside.

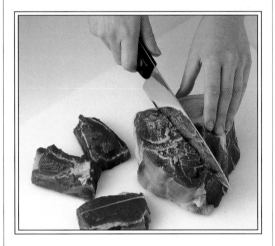

2 Cut the bones from the meat, and chop into large chunks. Place the meat and the bones into a large saucepan or stock pot. Add the caramelized onion with the ginger, star anise, bay leaf, cloves, fennel seeds and cassia bark or cinnamon stick.

3 Add the water, bring to the boil, reduce the heat and simmer gently for 2–3 hours, skimming off the fat and white froth from time to time.

4 Using a slotted spoon, remove the meat from the stock; when cool enough to handle, cut into small pieces, discarding the bones. Strain the stock and return to the pan or stock pot together with the meat. Bring back to the boil and season with the fish sauce and lime juice.

5 Slice the fillet steak very thinly and then chill until required. Place the accompaniments in separate bowls so that everyone can help themselves.

6 Cook the noodles in a large saucepan of boiling water until just tender. Drain and divide among individual serving bowls. Arrange the thinly sliced steak over the noodles and pour the hot stock on top.

THAI CHICKEN SOUP

A spicy light soup sweetened with coconut and crunchy peanut butter for added bite.

INGREDIENTS
15ml/1 tbsp vegetable oil
1 garlic clove, finely chopped
2 x 175g/6oz boned chicken breasts,
skinned and chopped
2.5ml/½ tsp ground turmeric
1.5ml/¼ tsp hot chilli powder
75g/3oz creamed coconut
900ml/1½ pints/3¾ cups hot
chicken stock
dash of lemon juice
30ml/2 tbsp crunchy peanut butter
50g/2oz/1 cup thread egg noodles, broken
into small pieces
15ml/1 tbsp spring onions,
finely chopped
15ml/1 tbsp chopped fresh coriander
salt and freshly ground black pepper
30ml/2 tbsp desiccated coconut and
½ fresh red chilli, seeded and finely
chopped, to garnish

SERVES 4

1 Heat the oil in a large pan and fry the garlic for 1 minute. Add the chicken and spices and stir-fry for a further 3–4 minutes.

2 Crumble the creamed coconut into the hot chicken stock and stir until dissolved. Pour this mixture on to the chicken and add the lemon juice, peanut butter and egg noodles.

3 Cover and simmer for about 15 minutes. Add the spring onions and fresh coriander, then season well with salt and freshly ground black pepper and cook for a further 5 minutes.

4 Meanwhile, place the coconut and chopped chilli in a small frying pan and heat for about 3 minutes, stirring frequently, until the coconut is lightly browned.

5 Pour the soup into individual bowls and sprinkle with the fried coconut and chopped chilli.

TAMARIND AND VEGETABLE SOUP

 ayur Assam is a colourful and refreshing soup from Jakarta with more than a hint of sharpness.

INGREDIENTS
FOR THE SPICE PASTE
5 shallots or 1 medium red onion, sliced
3 garlic cloves, crushed
2.5cm/1in lengkuas, *peeled and sliced*
1–2 fresh red chillies, seeded and sliced
25g/1oz raw peanuts
1cm/½in cube terasi, *prepared*
1.2 litres/2 pints/5 cups
well-flavoured stock
50–75g/2–3oz salted peanuts,
lightly crushed
15–30ml/1–2 tbsp dark brown sugar
5ml/1 tsp tamarind pulp, soaked in
75ml/5 tbsp warm water for 15 minutes
salt
1 fresh green chilli, sliced, to garnish

FOR THE VEGETABLES
1 chayote, thinly peeled, seeds removed,
flesh finely sliced
115g/4oz French beans, trimmed and
finely sliced
50g/2oz/¼ cup sweetcorn kernels
handful green leaves, such as watercress,
rocket or Chinese leaves, finely shredded

SERVES 4

1 Prepare the spice paste by grinding the shallots or onion, garlic, *lengkuas,* chillies, raw peanuts and *terasi* to a paste in a food processor or with a pestle and mortar.

2 Pour in some of the stock to moisten and then pour this mixture into a pan or wok, adding the rest of the stock. Cook for 15 minutes with the lightly crushed peanuts and sugar.

3 Strain the tamarind, discarding the seeds, and reserve the juice.

4 About 5 minutes before serving, add the chayote slices, beans and sweetcorn to the soup and cook fairly rapidly. At the last minute, add the green leaves and salt to taste.

5 Add the tamarind juice and taste for seasoning. Serve, garnished with slices of green chilli.

CHICKEN KOFTA BALTI WITH PANEER

Paneer is sometimes known as "Indian cheese". It is popular as a red meat substitute, as it is rich in protein and relatively low in fat.

INGREDIENTS
FOR THE KOFTAS
450g/1lb chicken, skinned,
boned and cubed
5ml/1 tsp garlic pulp
5ml/1 tsp shredded ginger
7.5ml/1½ tsp ground coriander
7.5ml/1½ tsp chilli powder
2.5ml/½ tsp ground fenugreek
1.5ml/¼ tsp turmeric
5ml/1 tsp salt
30ml/2 tbsp chopped fresh coriander
2 fresh green chillies, chopped
600ml/1 pint/2½ cups water
corn oil for frying
mint sprigs and red chilli,
crushed and dried, to garnish

FOR THE PANEER MIXTURE
1 medium onion, sliced
1 red pepper, seeded and cut into strips
1 green pepper, seeded and cut into strips
175g/6oz paneer, cubed
175g/6oz/¾ cup sweetcorn

SERVES 6

1 Put all the kofta ingredients, apart from the oil and garnishes into a saucepan. Bring to the boil slowly, over a medium heat, and cook until all the liquid has evaporated.

2 Remove from the heat and allow to cool slightly. Put the mixture into a food processor or blender and process for about 2 minutes, stopping once or twice to loosen the mixture with a spoon.

3 Scrape the mixture into a large mixing bowl using a wooden spoon. Taking a little of the mixture at a time, shape it into small balls using your hands. You should be able to make about 12 koftas.

4 Heat some oil in a karahi, wok or a deep round-bottomed frying pan over a high heat. When the oil begins to smoke, turn the heat down slightly and tip four koftas carefully into the oil. Move them around gently to ensure that they cook evenly.

5 When the koftas are lightly browned remove them from the oil with a slotted spoon and drain on kitchen paper. Set to one side. Repeat with the remaining koftas.

6 Heat up some more oil in the karahi, and briefly fry all the ingredients needed for the paneer mixture. This should take about 3 minutes over a high heat.

7 Divide the paneer mixture into 6 equal portions. Add the koftas to each serving, and garnish with mint sprigs and the crushed red chilli, if wished.

PORK SATÉ

This Indonesian dish is known as *Saté Babi Ketjap*. Although Indonesia is a Muslim country, there have been waves of Chinese immigrants who have made an enormous contribution to its cuisine, including the introduction of pork in many recipes. However, beef or lamb works just as well.

INGREDIENTS
500g/1¼ lb pork fillet
lime wedges, to garnish

FOR THE MARINADE
150ml/¼ pint/⅔ cup dark soy sauce
3–4 garlic cloves, crushed
45ml/3 tbsp groundnut oil
50g/2oz peanuts, finely crushed
(optional)
salt and freshly ground black pepper

FOR THE SAUCE
1 onion, finely chopped
2–3 fresh red chillies, seeded and ground
75ml/5 tbsp dark soy sauce
60–90ml/4–6 tbsp water
juice of 1–2 limes or 1 large lemon
50g/2oz peanuts, coarsely ground

SERVES 12

1 Wipe and trim the meat. Cut the pork into 2.5cm/1in cubes or into thin strips about 1cm/½in wide by 5cm/2in long.

2 Blend the dark soy sauce, garlic and oil together with the seasoning and the crushed peanuts, if using. Pour this mixture over the meat and allow to marinate for at least 1 hour, turning in the marinade from time to time.

3 If using wooden or bamboo skewers, soak them in water for 1 hour so that they don't burn when the satés are cooking. Then thread three or four pieces of meat on to one end of each skewer.

4 Make the sauce. Put the onion, chillies, soy sauce and water in a saucepan. Bring to the boil, and then simmer gently for 4–5 minutes. Cool, then stir in the freshly squeezed lime or lemon juice.

5 Add the ground peanuts to the sauce just before serving. Preheat the grill or barbecue.

6 Cook the satés, turning frequently for about 5–8 minutes, until tender. Garnish with lime wedges and serve with the sauce.

VIETNAMESE SPRING ROLLS

Crunchy spring rolls are the perfect starter, complemented here by *nuoc cham* sauce.

INGREDIENTS
6 dried Chinese mushrooms, soaked
225g/8oz lean ground pork
115g/4oz uncooked prawns, peeled,
deveined and chopped
115g/4oz white crabmeat, picked over
1 carrot, shredded
50g/2oz cellophane noodles, soaked in
water, drained and cut into short lengths
4 spring onions, finely sliced
2 garlic cloves, finely chopped
30ml/2 tbsp fish sauce
juice of 1 lime
freshly ground black pepper
25 x 10cm/4in Vietnamese rice sheets
oil, for deep frying

FOR THE SAUCE
2 garlic cloves, finely chopped
30ml/2 tbsp white wine vinegar
juice of 1 lime
30ml/2 tbsp sugar
120ml/4fl oz/1/2 cup fish sauce
120ml/4fl oz/1/2 cup water
2 red chillies, seeded and chopped

MAKES 25

1 Drain the mushrooms. Remove and discard the stems and slice the caps into a bowl. Add the pork, prawns, crabmeat, carrot, noodles, spring onions and garlic.

2 Season with the fish sauce, lime juice and pepper. Set the mixture aside for 30 minutes to allow the flavours to blend.

3 Meanwhile make the *nuoc cham* sauce. Mix together the garlic, vinegar, lime juice, sugar, fish sauce, water and chillies in a serving bowl, then cover and set aside.

4 Assemble the spring rolls. Brush a rice sheet with warm water until pliable. Place 10ml/2 tsp of the filling near the edge of the sheet. Fold the sides over the filling, fold in the two ends, then roll up, sealing the ends with a little water.

5 Make more rolls until all the filling is used up. Then heat the oil for deep frying to 180°C/350°F or until a cube of dry bread added to the oil browns in 30–45 seconds. Add the rolls, a few at a time, and fry until golden brown and crisp. Drain on kitchen paper. Serve hot, garnished with lettuce, cucumber, radish and coriander, if desired. Offer the *nuoc cham* sauce in a separate bowl.

FISH CAKES WITH CUCUMBER RELISH

hese delicate Thai fish cakes are a familiar and popular appetizer, often sold at pavement stalls.

INGREDIENTS
*300g/11oz white fish fillet, such as cod,
cut into chunks
30ml/2 tbsp red curry paste
1 egg
30ml/2 tbsp fish sauce
5ml/1 tsp granulated sugar
30ml/2 tbsp cornflour
3 kaffir lime leaves, shredded
15ml/1 tbsp chopped coriander
50g/2oz green beans, finely sliced
oil for frying
Chinese mustard cress, to garnish*

FOR THE CUCUMBER RELISH
*60ml/4 tbsp Thai coconut or rice vinegar
60ml/4 tbsp water
50g/2oz sugar
1 head pickled garlic
1 cucumber, quartered and sliced
4 shallots, finely sliced
15ml/1 tbsp root ginger, finely chopped
red chillies, seeded and chopped,
to garnish*

MAKES 12

1 To make the relish, bring the vinegar, water and sugar to the boil. Stir until the sugar dissolves completely, then remove from the heat to cool.

2 Combine the pickled garlic, sliced cucumber, shallots and root ginger together in a bowl and pour over the cooled vinegar mixture. Garnish with chillies.

3 Combine the fish, curry paste and egg in a food processor and process well. Transfer the mixture to a bowl, add the rest of the ingredients, except for the oil and cress and mix well.

4 Mould and shape the fish mixture into cakes about 5cm/2in in diameter and 5mm/¼in thick.

5 Heat the oil in a wok and fry the cakes, a few at a time, for about 4–5 minutes. Remove and drain on kitchen paper. Garnish with cress and serve with the relish.

RENDANG

This popular Indonesian dish is often served with deep-fried onions and plain boiled rice.

INGREDIENTS

1kg/2¼lb prime beef in one piece
2 onions or 5–6 shallots, sliced
4 garlic cloves, crushed
2.5cm/1in fresh lengkuas, peeled and sliced, or 5ml/1 tsp lengkuas powder
2.5cm/1in fresh root ginger, peeled and sliced
4–6 fresh red chillies, seeded and sliced
1 lemon grass stem, lower part, sliced
2.5cm/1in fresh turmeric, peeled and sliced, or 5ml/1 tsp ground turmeric
5ml/1 tsp coriander seeds, dry-fried and ground
5ml/1 tsp cumin seeds, dry-fried and ground
2 kaffir lime leaves
5ml/1 tsp tamarind pulp, soaked in 60ml/4 tbsp warm water
2 x 400ml/14fl oz cans coconut milk
300ml/½ pint/1¼ cups water
30ml/2 tbsp dark soy sauce
6–8 small new potatoes, scrubbed
salt
boiled rice and deep-fried onions, to serve

SERVES 6 – 8

1 Cut the meat in long strips and then into even-size pieces and place in a bowl.

2 Process the onions or shallots, crushed garlic, *lengkuas* or *lengkuas* powder, sliced ginger, chopped and deseeded chillies, sliced lemon grass and the fresh or ground turmeric to a fine paste in a food processor. Alternatively, grind finely together using a pestle and mortar.

COOK'S TIP
This dish tastes even better and more flavoursome if cooked a day in advance. Follow the recipe up to the end of Step 5; on the next day reheat and add the potatoes and seasoning.

3 Add the paste to the meat with the coriander and cumin and mix well. Tear the lime leaves and add them to the mixture. Cover and leave in a cool place to marinate while you prepare the other ingredients.

4 Strain the tamarind and reserve the juice. Pour the coconut milk, water and tamarind juice into a wok or flameproof casserole and stir in the spiced meat and soy sauce. Add seasoning as desired.

5 Stir until the liquid comes to the boil; then reduce the heat and simmer gently, half-covered, for about 1½–2 hours or until the meat is tender and the liquid reduced.

6 Add the potatoes 20–25 minutes before the end of the cooking time. Add a little more water to the pot. Season to taste and serve with rice and deep-fried onions.

STIR-FRIED BEEF IN OYSTER SAUCE

Another simple but delicious recipe. In Thailand, fresh straw mushrooms are readily available; if you can't get hold of them oyster mushrooms make a good substitute.

INGREDIENTS
450g/1lb rump steak
30ml/2 tbsp soy sauce
15ml/1 tbsp cornflour
45ml/3 tbsp vegetable oil
15ml/1 tbsp chopped garlic
15ml/1 tbsp chopped root ginger
225g/8oz mixed mushrooms, such as
shiitake, oyster and straw
30ml/2 tbsp oyster sauce
5ml/1 tsp granulated sugar
4 spring onions, cut into short lengths
freshly ground black pepper
2 red chillies, cut into strips, to garnish

SERVES 4 – 6

1 Slice the beef on the diagonal into long thin strips. Mix the soy sauce and cornflour together in a large bowl, stir in the beef and leave to marinate for 1–2 hours.

2 Heat half the oil in a wok or heavy-bottomed frying pan. Add the garlic and ginger and fry until fragrant. Stir in the beef. Stir to separate the strips, let them colour and then cook for 1–2 minutes. Remove from the pan and set aside.

3 Heat the remaining oil in the wok or frying pan. Add the shiitake, oyster and straw mushrooms. Cook until tender.

4 Return the beef to the wok with the mushrooms. Add the oyster sauce, sugar and freshly ground black pepper to taste. Mix well.

5 Add the spring onions; mix well. Serve garnished with strips of red chilli.

TANDOORI CHICKEN

T his classic Indian dish is traditionally cooked in the tandoor: a clay oven, heated by a charcoal or wood fire.

INGREDIENTS
8 chicken pieces, such as thighs,
drumsticks, or halved breasts, skinned
60ml/4 tbsp lemon juice
5ml/1 tsp salt
2 garlic cloves, roughly chopped
2.5cm/1in piece root ginger,
roughly chopped
2 green chillies, roughly chopped
175ml/6fl oz/¾ cup natural yogurt
5ml/1 tsp salt
5ml/1 tsp chilli powder
5ml/1 tsp garam masala
5ml/1 tsp ground cumin
5ml/1 tsp ground coriander
red food colouring (optional)
30ml/2 tbsp butter, melted
chilli powder, slice of lime and a sprig of
fresh mint, to garnish
green salad and red onion rings, to serve

SERVES 4

1 Cut deep slashes in the chicken pieces. Mix together the lemon juice and the salt and pour over the chicken. Leave to marinate for 10 minutes.

2 For the marinade, blend the garlic, ginger and chillies until smooth. Add to a bowl containing the yogurt, salt, chilli powder, garam masala, coriander and cumin and mix well. Brush the marinade over the chicken.

3 Coat the chicken with red food colouring using, if using. Cover the dish with a cloth and leave overnight to let the marinade soak into the chicken. Preheat the oven to 220°C/425°F/Gas 7. Put the chicken in a roasting tin, pour over the melted butter and bake for 40 minutes. Garnish with chilli powder, a twist of lime and sprigs of fresh mint. Serve with a mixed green salad and raw red onion rings.

BALTI LAMB WITH SPINACH

L amb with spinach, or *Saag Goshth*, is a well known recipe from the Punjab. It is important to use red peppers in this dish, as they add the distinctive flavour. This dish is best served with plain boiled rice or naan bread.

INGREDIENTS
5ml/1 tsp ginger pulp
5ml/1 tsp garlic pulp
7.5ml/1½ tsp chilli powder
5ml/1 tsp salt
5ml/1 tsp garam masala
90ml/6 tbsp corn oil
2 medium onions, sliced
675g/1½ lb lean lamb,
cut into 5cm/2in cubes
600–900ml/1–1½ pints/2½–3¾
cups water
400g/14oz fresh spinach
1 large red pepper, seeded and chopped
3 fresh green chillies, chopped
45ml/3 tbsp chopped fresh coriander
15ml/1 tbsp lemon juice

SERVES 4 – 6

1 Mix together the ginger, garlic, chilli powder, salt and garam masala in a bowl. Set to one side.

2 Heat the oil in a medium saucepan. Add the onions and fry for 10–12 minutes or until well browned.

3 Add the cubed lamb to the sizzling onions and stir-fry for about 2 minutes.

4 Tip in the spice mixture and stir well until the meat is thoroughly coated.

5 Pour in the water and bring to the boil. As soon as the water boils, cover the pan and lower the heat. Cook gently on a low heat for 25–35 minutes, or until the meat is tender, taking care not to let the contents of the pan burn.

6 If there is still a lot of water left in the pan when the meat has become tender, remove the lid and boil briskly to evaporate any excess.

7 Meanwhile, wash and chop the spinach roughly before blanching it for 1 minute in a pan of boiling water. Drain well.

8 Add the spinach to the lamb as soon as the water has evaporated. Fry over a medium heat for 7–10 minutes, using a wooden spoon in a semi-circular motion, scraping the bottom of the pan as you stir.

9 Add the red pepper, green chillies and fresh coriander to the pan and stir over a medium heat for 2 minutes. Sprinkle on the lemon juice and serve immediately.

COOK'S TIP
Frozen spinach can also be used for this dish, but try to find whole leaf spinach rather than the chopped kind. Allow the frozen spinach to thaw, then drain well; there is no need to blanch it.

BALINESE SPICED DUCK

D uck is a popular ingredient all over Asia. Cooked Balinese-style, in coconut milk and spices, it is deliciously moist and tender.

INGREDIENTS

8 duck portions, fat trimmed and reserved
50g/2oz/¼ cup desiccated coconut
175ml/6fl oz/¾ cup coconut milk
salt and freshly ground black pepper
deep-fried onions, to garnish
salad and chopped herbs, to serve

FOR THE SPICE PASTE

1 small onion or 4–6 shallots, sliced
2 garlic cloves, sliced
1cm/½in fresh root ginger,
peeled and sliced
1cm/½in fresh lengkuas,
peeled and sliced
2.5cm/1in fresh turmeric or 2.5ml/½ tsp
ground turmeric
1–2 red chillies, seeded and sliced
4 macadamia nuts or 8 almonds
5ml/1 tsp coriander seeds, dry-fried

SERVES 4

1 Place the duck fat trimmings in a heated frying pan, without oil, and allow the fat to drip off. Reserve the fat.

2 Fry the desiccated coconut in a preheated pan without oil, until crisp and brown in colour.

3 To make the spice paste, blend the onion or shallots, garlic, ginger, *lengkuas*, fresh or ground turmeric, chillies, nuts and coriander seeds to a paste in a food processor or with a pestle and mortar.

4 Spread half the spice paste over the duck portions and leave to marinate in a cool place for 3–4 hours. Preheat the oven to 160°C/325°F/Gas 3. Transfer the duck breasts to an oiled roasting tin. Cover with a double layer of foil and cook the duck in the oven for about 2 hours. When cooked, remove the duck from the pan and set aside to keep warm. Reserve the fat and juices from the duck and keep in the pan.

5 Turn the oven temperature up to 190°C/375°F/Gas 5. Heat the reserved duck fat in a pan, add the remaining spice paste and fry for 1–2 minutes. Stir in the coconut milk and simmer for 2 minutes. Cover the duck with the spice mixture and sprinkle with the fried coconut. Cook in the oven for 20–30 minutes.

6 Arrange the duck on a platter and garnish with deep-fried onions. Season to taste and serve with the salad and herbs.

CHICKEN BIRYANI

This popular dish can be found in Indian restaurants the world over. It is simple to make at home.

INGREDIENTS

275g/10oz/1½ cups basmati rice, rinsed
2.5ml/½ tsp salt
5 whole cardamom pods
2–3 whole cloves
1 cinnamon stick
45ml/3 tbsp vegetable oil
3 onions, sliced
675g/1½ lb boneless, skinned chicken
(4 x 175g/6oz chicken breasts), cubed
1.5ml/¼ tsp hot chilli powder
5ml/1 tsp ground cumin
5ml/1 tsp ground coriander
2.5ml/½ tsp freshly ground black pepper
3 garlic cloves, finely chopped
5ml/1 tsp finely chopped fresh root ginger
juice of 1 lemon
4 tomatoes, sliced
30ml/2 tbsp chopped fresh coriander
150ml/¼ pint/⅔ cup natural yogurt
2.5ml/½ tsp saffron strands soaked
in 10ml/2 tsp hot milk
45ml/3 tbsp/¼ cup toasted halved
almonds, fresh coriander sprigs and
natural yogurt, to serve

SERVES 4

1 Preheat the oven to 190°C/375°F/Gas 5. Bring a pan of water to the boil and add the rice, salt, cardamom pods, cloves and cinnamon stick. Boil for 2 minutes and then drain, leaving the whole spices in the rice.

2 Heat the oil in a pan and fry the onions for 8 minutes, until browned. Add the chicken followed by all the ground spices, the garlic, ginger and lemon juice. Stir-fry for 5 minutes.

3 Transfer the chicken mixture to an ovenproof casserole and lay the tomato slices on top. Sprinkle over the chopped fresh coriander and spoon over the yogurt, completely covering the meat and tomatoes. Top with the drained rice.

4 Drizzle the saffron and milk mixture over the rice and pour over 150ml/¼ pint/ ⅔ cup of water.

5 Cover tightly and bake in the oven for 1 hour. Transfer to a warmed serving platter and remove the whole spices from the rice. Garnish with toasted almonds and fresh coriander and serve with yogurt.

RED CHICKEN CURRY WITH BAMBOO SHOOTS

amboo shoots lend a crunchy texture to this classic Asian dish.

INGREDIENTS
1 litre/1¾ pints/4 cups coconut milk
450g/1lb diced boneless chicken
30ml/2 tbsp fish sauce
15ml/1 tbsp granulated sugar
225g/8oz bamboo shoots, sliced
5 kaffir lime leaves, torn
salt and freshly ground black pepper
chillies, basil and mint leaves, to garnish

FOR THE RED CURRY PASTE
12–15 red chillies, seeded
4 shallots, thinly sliced
2 garlic cloves, chopped
15ml/1 tbsp chopped galangal
2 stalks lemon grass, chopped
3 kaffir lime leaves, chopped
4 coriander roots
10 black peppercorns
5ml/1 tsp coriander seeds
2.5ml/½ tsp cumin seeds
good pinch of ground cinnamon
5ml/1 tsp ground turmeric
2.5ml/½ tsp shrimp paste
5ml/1 tsp salt
30ml/2 tbsp oil

SERVES 4 – 6

1 For the red curry paste, combine the all the ingredients in a pestle and mortar except for the oil, and pound until smooth.

2 Add the oil a little at a time and blend in well. Place in a jar in the refrigerator until ready to use. It will keep for 2 weeks.

3 In a large heavy-based saucepan, bring half the coconut milk to the boil, stirring until it separates.

4 Add 30ml/2 tbsp red curry paste and cook for a few minutes.

5 Add the chicken, fish sauce and sugar. Fry for 3–5 minutes until the chicken changes colour, stirring constantly to prevent it from sticking to the pan.

6 Add the rest of the coconut milk, bamboo shoots and lime leaves. Return to the boil. Season to taste. Serve garnished with chillies, basil and mint leaves.

COOK'S TIP
It is quite acceptable to use canned bamboo, if fresh bamboo is not available. Whenever possible, buy whole canned bamboo, as it is generally crisper and of better quality than sliced shoots.

KASHMIR COCONUT FISH

Fish and coconut are a popular combination in Asian cooking. This deliciously sweet curry is from the northern region of India.

INGREDIENTS
30ml/2 tbsp vegetable oil
2 onions, sliced
1 green pepper, seeded and sliced
1 garlic clove, crushed
1 dried chilli, seeded and chopped
5ml/1 tsp ground coriander
5ml/1 tsp ground cumin
2.5ml/¹⁄₂ tsp ground turmeric
2.5ml/¹⁄₂ tsp hot chilli powder
2.5ml/¹⁄₂ tsp garam masala
15ml/1 tbsp plain flour
115g/4oz/1¹⁄₃ cups creamed coconut
675g/1¹⁄₂lb haddock fillet,
skinned and chopped
4 tomatoes, skinned, seeded and chopped
15ml/1 tbsp lemon juice
30ml/2 tbsp ground almonds
30ml/2 tbsp double cream
salt and freshly ground black pepper
fresh coriander sprigs, to garnish
naan bread and rice, to serve

SERVES 4

1 Heat the oil in a large saucepan and add the onions, pepper and garlic. Cook for 6–7 minutes, until the onions and peppers have softened. Stir in the chopped dried chilli, all the ground spices, the chilli powder, garam masala and flour, and cook for 1 minute.

2 Dissolve the creamed coconut in 600ml/1 pint/2¹⁄₂ cups boiling water and stir into the spicy vegetable mixture. Bring to the boil, cover and then simmer gently for 6 minutes.

3 Add the fish and tomatoes and cook for about 5–6 minutes, or until the fish has turned opaque. Uncover and gently stir in the lemon juice, ground almonds and cream. Season well and garnish with coriander. Serve with naan bread and rice.

COOK'S TIP
You can replace the haddock with other firm-fleshed white fish, such as cod or whiting, or even stir in a few cooked peeled prawns, if liked.

GREEN PRAWN CURRY

A fragrant, creamy curry from Thailand that takes very little time to prepare. It can also be made with thin strips of chicken meat.

INGREDIENTS

30ml/2 tbsp vegetable oil
30ml/2 tbsp green curry paste
450g/1lb king prawns,
shelled and deveined
4 kaffir lime leaves, torn
1 stalk lemon grass, bruised and chopped
250ml/8fl oz/1 cup coconut milk
½ cucumber, seeded and cut into
thin batons
10–15 basil leaves
30ml/2 tbsp fish sauce
4 green chillies, sliced to garnish

SERVES 4 – 6

1 Heat the oil in a frying pan. Add the green curry paste and fry until bubbling and fragrant.

2 Add the prawns, lime leaves and lemon grass. Fry for 1–2 minutes, until the prawns are pink.

3 Stir in the coconut milk and bring to a gentle boil. Simmer, stirring occasionally, for 5 minutes or until the prawns are tender.

4 Stir in the cucumber and basil and add the fish sauce. Garnish with the sliced green chillies, and serve.

CHILLI CRABS

I t is possible to find variations on *Kepitang Pedas*, as it's called in Indonesia, all over Asia.

INGREDIENTS

2 cooked crabs, about 675g/1½lb
1cm/½in cube terasi
2 garlic cloves
2 fresh red chillies, seeded, or 5ml/1 tsp
chopped chilli from a jar
2.5cm/1in fresh root ginger,
peeled and sliced
60ml/4 tbsp sunflower oil
300ml/½ pint/1¼ cups tomato ketchup
15ml/1 tbsp dark brown sugar
150ml/¼ pint/⅔ cup warm water
4 spring onions, chopped, to garnish
cucumber chunks and hot toast,
to serve (optional)

SERVES 4

1 Remove the large claws of one crab and turn it on to its back, with the head facing away from you. Push the body up from the main shell. Discard the stomach sac, lungs and any green matter. Leave the brown meat in the shell and cut in half with a cleaver. Cut the body section in half and crack the claws with a sharp blow from a hammer or cleaver. Avoid splintering the claws. Repeat with the other crab.

2 Grind the *terasi*, garlic, chillies and ginger to a paste in a food processor or with a pestle and mortar.

3 Heat a wok or heavy-based pan and add the oil. Fry the spice paste, stirring it all the time, without browning.

4 Stir in the tomato ketchup, sugar and water and mix well. When just boiling, add the crab pieces and toss in the sauce until well coated and hot. Serve in a large bowl, sprinkled with the chopped spring onions. Place in the centre of the table for everyone to help themselves. Accompany with cucumber chunks and hot toast, if using, for mopping up the sauce.

MALAYSIAN FISH CURRY

his potent curry, known as *Ikan Moolee,* is often served with Hot Tomato Sambal and plain rice.

INGREDIENTS

*675g/1¹/₂ lb monkfish, hokey
or red snapper fillet
45ml/3 tbsp freshly grated
or shredded coconut
30ml/2 tbsp vegetable oil
1 piece galangal or fresh ginger,
2.5cm/1in long, peeled and thinly sliced
2 small red chillies, seeded
and finely chopped
2 cloves garlic, crushed
1 piece lemon grass,
5cm/2in long, shredded
1 piece shrimp paste, 1cm/¹/₂in square,
or 15ml/1 tbsp fish sauce
400ml/14fl oz/1²/₃ cups canned
coconut milk
600ml/1 pint/2¹/₂ cups chicken stock
2.5ml/¹/₂ tsp turmeric
15ml/1 tbsp sugar
juice of 1 lime or ¹/₂ lemon
salt
chunks of lime, freshly chopped coriander,
and Hot Tomato Sambal, to serve*

SERVES 4 – 6

1 Cut the fish into large chunks, season with salt and set aside.

2 Dry-fry the coconut in a wok until evenly brown. Add the oil, *galangal* or ginger, chillies, garlic and lemon grass and fry briefly. Stir in the shrimp paste or fish sauce. Strain the coconut milk through a sieve, and add the thin coconut liquid.

3 Add the chicken stock, turmeric, sugar, a little salt and the lime or lemon juice. Simmer for 10 minutes. Add the fish and simmer for a further 6–8 minutes. Stir in the solid coconut milk, simmer gently to thicken. Transfer to a large bowl. Decorate with chunks of lime and coriander to serve.

THAI PRAWN SALAD

his salad has the distinctive flavour of lemon grass, an ingredient used widely in South-east Asian cooking.

INGREDIENTS

250g/9oz cooked, peeled
extra large tiger prawns
15ml/1 tbsp fish sauce
30ml/2 tbsp lime juice
2.5ml/½ tsp soft light brown sugar
1 small fresh red chilli, finely chopped
1 spring onion, finely chopped
1 small garlic clove, crushed
2.5cm/1in piece fresh lemon grass,
finely chopped
30ml/2 tbsp chopped fresh coriander
45ml/3 tbsp dry white wine
8–12 lettuce leaves, to serve
fresh coriander sprigs, to garnish

SERVES 4

1 Place the prawns in a bowl and add the fish sauce, lime juice, sugar, chilli, spring onion, garlic and lemon grass. Stir together and then add the coriander and wine. Stir well, cover and leave to marinate in the refrigerator for 2–3 hours until the flavours have permeated the prawns. Mix and turn the prawns from time to time, so that they are evenly coated.

2 Arrange two or three of the lettuce leaves on to four serving plates.

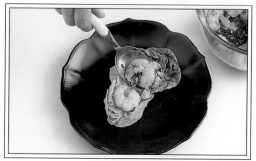

3 Spoon the prawn salad into the lettuce leaves. Garnish with fresh coriander and serve at once.

PRAWN AND PANEER BALTI

Paneer is an excellent red meat substitute, available at many Asian stores. It can be easily made at home (see Cook's Tip).

INGREDIENTS
12 cooked king prawns
175g/6oz paneer
30ml/2 tbsp tomato purée
60ml/4 tbsp Greek-style yogurt
2.5ml/½ tsp garam masala
5ml/1 tsp chilli powder
5ml/1 tsp garlic pulp
5ml/1 tsp salt
10ml/2 tsp mango powder
5ml/1 tsp ground coriander
115g/4oz/8 tbsp butter
15ml/1 tbsp corn oil
3 fresh green chillies, chopped
45ml/3 tbsp chopped fresh coriander
150ml/¼ pint/⅔ cup single cream

SERVES 4

1 Peel the king prawns and cut the paneer into small cubes.

2 Blend the tomato purée, yogurt, garam masala, chilli powder, garlic, salt, mango powder and ground coriander in a mixing bowl and set to one side.

3 Melt the butter and oil in a deep round-bottomed frying pan. Lower the heat, add the prawns and paneer in batches, and stir-fry for about 2 minutes. Remove with a slotted spoon and drain on kitchen paper.

4 Pour the spice mixture into the fat left in the pan and stir-fry for about 1 minute.

5 Add the paneer and prawns, and cook for 7–10 minutes, stirring occasionally, until the prawns are heated through.

6 Add the fresh chillies and most of the coriander, and pour in the cream. Heat through for about 2 minutes, garnish with the remaining coriander and serve.

COOK'S TIP
To make paneer, boil 1 litre/1¾ pints/4 cups milk. Add 10ml/2 tsp lemon juice, stirring constantly until the milk thickens and curdles. Strain through a muslin-lined sieve. Press under a heavy weight until flat. Make the day before you plan to use it; it will then be firm and manageable.

INDIAN PILAU RICE

Pilau rice is the perfect partner to many Asian main courses, and the versatile base of many side dishes.

INGREDIENTS
225g/8oz/1¼ cups basmati rice, rinsed well
30ml/2 tbsp vegetable oil
1 small onion, finely chopped
1 garlic clove, crushed
5ml/1 tsp fennel seeds
15ml/1 tbsp sesame seeds
2.5ml/½ tsp ground turmeric
5ml/1 tsp ground cumin
1.5ml/¼ tsp salt
2 whole cloves
4 cardamom pods, lightly crushed
5 black peppercorns
450ml/¾ pint/1⅞ cups chicken stock
15ml/1 tbsp ground almonds
fresh coriander sprigs, to garnish
beansprout salad, to serve

SERVES 4

1 Soak the rice in cold water for about 30 minutes. Heat the oil in a saucepan, add the onion and garlic, and fry gently for 5 minutes, until softened.

2 Stir in the fennel and sesame seeds, the turmeric, cumin, salt, cloves, cardamom pods and peppercorns and fry for about a minute. Drain the rice well, add to the pan and stir-fry for a further 3 minutes.

3 Pour on the chicken stock. Bring to the boil, cover and reduce the heat to very low. Simmer gently for 20 minutes, without removing the lid until all the liquid has been completely absorbed.

4 Remove from the heat and leave to stand for 2–3 minutes. Separate the grains with a fork and stir in the ground almonds. Garnish with coriander sprigs and serve with the beansprout salad.

COOK'S TIP
A variety of vegetables can be added to this recipe to make a tasty vegetarian main course: for Pea and Mushroom Pilau, add a medium tomato and 50g/2oz/ ⅔ cup button mushrooms to the saucepan after Step 2. After 15 minutes cooking time, add 75g/ 3oz/⅓ cup petit pois to the pan. Continue with Steps 3 and 4.

INDONESIAN PORK AND PRAWN RICE

Nasi Goreng is one of the most familiar and well-loved Indonesian dishes. It is a marvellous way to use up leftover rice, chicken and other meats such as pork. It is important that the rice is cold and the grains are separated before adding the other ingredients, so it is best to cook the rice the day before.

INGREDIENTS

350g/12oz/1½ cups long-grain rice, such
as basmati, cooked and left until cold
2 eggs
30ml/2 tbsp water
105ml/7 tbsp oil
225g/8oz pork fillet or fillet of beef
115g/4oz cooked, peeled prawns
175g–225g/6–8oz cooked
chicken, chopped
2–3 fresh red chillies, seeded and sliced
1cm/½in cube terasi
2 garlic cloves, crushed
1 onion, sliced
30ml/2 tbsp dark soy sauce or
45–60ml/3–4 tbsp tomato ketchup
salt and freshly ground black pepper
celery leaves, deep-fried onions and
coriander sprigs, to garnish

SERVES 4 – 6

1 Cook and cool the rice. Fork it through to separate the grains and keep it in a covered pan or dish until required.

2 Beat the eggs. Add the seasoning and water and make two or three omelettes in a frying pan, with a small amount of oil. Roll up each omelette, leave to cool, and cut in strips when cold. Set aside.

3 Cut the pork or beef into neat strips and put the meat, prawns and chicken pieces into separate bowls. Shred one of the chillies and reserve it.

4 Put the terasi, with the remaining chilli, garlic and onion in a food processor and grind to a fine paste. Alternatively, pound together using a pestle and mortar.

5 Fry the paste in the remaining hot oil, without browning, until it gives off a rich, spicy aroma, for about 3 minutes. Add the pork or beef, tossing the meat all the time, to seal in the juices. Cook for 2 minutes, stirring constantly.

6 Add the prawns, cook for a further 2 minutes, and then stir in the chicken, cold rice, dark soy sauce or ketchup and season to taste. Stir all the time to keep the rice light and fluffy and prevent it from sticking to the pan.

7 Turn the rice mixture on to a hot platter and garnish with the omelette strips, celery leaves, deep-fried onions, reserved shredded chilli and the fresh, chopped coriander sprigs.

SPECIAL FRIED NOODLES

Mee Goreng is perhaps the most well-known dish of Singapore, and several other Asian countries have their own versions of this versatile dish.

INGREDIENTS
275g/10oz egg noodles
1 skinless chicken breast
115g/4oz lean pork
30ml/2 tbsp vegetable oil
150g/5oz prawn tails, fresh or cooked
4 shallots, or 1 medium onion, chopped
1 piece fresh ginger 1cm/½in long,
peeled and thinly sliced
2 cloves garlic, crushed
45ml/3 tbsp light soy sauce
5–10ml/1–2 tsp chilli sauce
15ml/1 tbsp rice wine
or white wine vinegar
10ml/2 tsp sugar
2.5ml/½ tsp salt
115ml/4oz white cabbage, shredded
115ml/4oz fresh spinach, shredded
3 spring onions, shredded

SERVES 4 – 6

1 Bring a large saucepan of salted water to the boil and cook the noodles according to the instructions on the packet. Drain and set aside. Place the chicken breast and pork in the freezer for about 30 minutes to firm but not freeze.

2 Slice the meat thinly against the grain. Heat the oil in a large wok and fry the chicken, pork and prawns for 2–3 minutes. Add the shallots or onion, ginger and garlic and fry without letting them colour.

3 Add the soy and chilli sauces, wine or vinegar, sugar and salt. Simmer, then add the cabbage, spinach and spring onions. Cover and cook for 3–4 minutes. Add the noodles, heat through and serve.

FRIED JASMINE RICE

T his dish uses Thai basil, or *Bai Grapao*, also known as Holy Basil, which has a unique, pungent flavour that is both spicy and sharp.

INGREDIENTS
45ml/3 tbsp vegetable oil
1 egg, beaten
1 onion, chopped
15ml/1 tbsp chopped garlic
15ml/1 tbsp shrimp paste
1kg/2¼lb/4 cups jasmine rice, cooked
350g/12oz cooked shelled prawns
50g/2oz/⅓ cup thawed frozen peas
oyster sauce, to taste
2 spring onions, chopped
15–20 Thai basil leaves, roughly snipped, plus an extra sprig to garnish

SERVES 4 – 6

1 Heat 15ml/1 tbsp of the oil in a wok or frying pan. Add the beaten egg and swirl it around the pan to set like a thin pancake.

2 Cook until golden, slide on to a board, roll and cut into thin strips. Set aside.

3 Heat the remaining oil, add the onion and garlic and fry for 2–3 minutes. Stir in the shrimp paste and mix well.

4 Add the cooked rice, prawns and peas. Toss and stir together, until everything is heated through.

5 Season with oyster sauce to taste; take care as it is very salty. Add the spring onions and basil leaves. Transfer to a serving dish and serve topped with the strips of egg pancake. Garnish with a sprig of basil.

SOFT FRIED NOODLES

 This basic, traditional dish is an ideal accompaniment for rich or spicy main courses.

INGREDIENTS
300g/11oz dried egg noodles
30ml/2 tbsp vegetable oil
30ml/2 tbsp finely chopped spring onions
soy sauce, to taste
salt and freshly ground black pepper
chopped spring onion, to garnish
deep-fried onion rings, to serve

SERVES 4 – 6

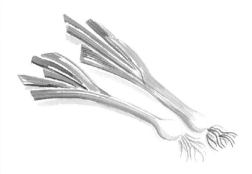

1 Cook the noodles in a large saucepan of boiling water until just tender, following the directions on the packet. Drain, rinse under cold running water to remove any excess starch, and drain again thoroughly.

2 Heat the oil in a wok and swirl it around. Add the spring onions and fry for about 30 seconds. Add the noodles, stirring gently to separate the strands.

3 Reduce the heat and fry the noodles, until they are lightly browned and crisp on the outside, but still soft on the inside.

4 Season with soy sauce, salt and freshly ground black pepper. Garnish with chopped spring onions and serve at once with deep-fried onion rings.

EGG FRIED NOODLES

Yellow bean sauce gives these noodles a savoury flavour. They are eaten all over Asia, accompanying many meat and vegetable dishes.

INGREDIENTS
350g/12oz medium-thick egg noodles
60ml/4 tbsp vegetable oil
4 spring onions, cut into
1cm/½in rounds
juice of 1 lime
15ml/1 tbsp soy sauce
2 garlic cloves, finely chopped
175g/6oz skinless, boneless chicken
breast, sliced
175g/6oz raw prawns,
peeled and deveined
175g/6oz squid, cleaned
and cut into rings
15ml/1 tbsp yellow bean sauce
15ml/1 tbsp fish sauce
15ml/1 tbsp soft light brown sugar
2 eggs
coriander leaves, to garnish

SERVES 4 – 6

1 Cook the noodles in a saucepan of boiling water until just tender, then drain well and set aside.

2 Heat half the oil in a wok or large frying pan. Add the spring onions, stir-fry for 2 minutes, then add the noodles, lime juice and soy sauce and stir-fry for a further 2–3 minutes. Transfer the mixture to a bowl, cover, and keep warm.

3 Heat the remaining oil in the wok or pan. Add the garlic, chicken, prawns and squid. Stir-fry over a high heat for about 5 minutes or until all the ingredients are cooked through.

4 Stir in the yellow bean sauce, fish sauce and sugar, then break the eggs into the mixture, one at a time, stirring gently until they set.

5 Add the noodles to the wok or pan. Mix all the ingredients together well, and heat through. Serve garnished with fresh coriander leaves.

FRUIT AND RAW VEGETABLE GADO-GADO

his tangy, fresh starter, is ideal before a spicy main course, or to accompany a creamy curry.

INGREDIENTS
2 unripe pears, peeled at the last moment
1–2 eating apples
juice of 1/2 lemon
1 small, crisp lettuce or a banana leaf
1/2 cucumber, seeded, sliced and salted, set aside for 15 minutes, then rinsed and drained
6 small tomatoes, cut into wedges
3 slices fresh pineapple, cored and cut into wedges
3 eggs or 12 quail's eggs, hard-boiled and shelled
175g/6oz egg noodles, cooked, cooled and chopped
deep-fried onions, to garnish

FOR THE PEANUT SAUCE
15ml/1 tbsp tamarind pulp
2–4 fresh red chillies, seeded and ground
300ml/1/2 pint/1 1/4 cups coconut milk
350g/12oz crunchy peanut butter
15ml/1 tbsp dark soy sauce
salt
coarsely crushed peanuts, to garnish

SERVES 6

1 To make the peanut sauce, soak the tamarind pulp in 45ml/3 tbsp warm water, strain and reserve the juice. Put the chillies and coconut milk in a saucepan. Add the peanut butter and heat gently, stirring, until smooth.

2 Allow to simmer gently until the sauce thickens, then add the soy sauce and the tamarind juice. Season with salt to taste. Pour into a bowl and garnish with a few coarsely crushed peanuts.

3 To make the salad, peel and core the pears and apples, slice them and sprinkle the apples with lemon juice. Shred the lettuce leaves to form a bed for the salad in a shallow bowl or flat platter. Alternatively line with the whole banana leaf. Arrange the fruit and vegetables attractively on top.

4 Add the sliced or quartered hard-boiled eggs (leave quail's eggs whole) and the chopped noodles. Garnish with the deep-fried onions.

5 Serve at once, accompanied with a bowl of the peanut sauce.

COOK'S TIP
Any fruit or vegetable can be substituted for the ones mentioned here. Experiment with soft, sweet tropical fruits such as mango or lychees, combined with sharp fruits such as grapefruit or lemon, for extra zing, and an authentic sweet and sour experience.

HOT AND SOUR CHICKEN SALAD

 delicious substantial salad from Vietnam, known as *Nuong Ngu Vi*, with a piquant peanut flavour.

INGREDIENTS
2 chicken breast fillets, skinned
1 small red chilli, seeded and finely chopped
1 piece fresh root ginger, 1cm/½in long, peeled and finely chopped
1 clove garlic, crushed
15ml/1 tbsp crunchy peanut butter
30ml/2 tbsp chopped coriander leaves
5ml/1 tsp sugar
2.5ml/½ tsp salt
15ml/1 tbsp rice or white wine vinegar
60ml/4 tbsp vegetable oil
10ml/2 tsp fish sauce (optional)

FOR THE SALAD
115g/4oz beansprouts
1 head Chinese leaves, roughly shredded
2 medium carrots, cut into thin sticks
1 red onion, cut into fine rings
2 large gherkins, sliced

SERVES 4 – 6

1 Slice the chicken thinly, place in a shallow bowl and set aside. Grind the chilli, ginger and garlic in a pestle and mortar. Transfer to a small bowl and add the peanut butter, coriander leaves, sugar and salt. Mix thoroughly.

2 Add the vinegar, 2 tablespoons of the oil and the fish sauce, if using, to the small bowl. Combine well. Brush this spice mixture all over the chicken strips and leave to marinate in a cool place for at least 2–3 hours, until the flavours have soaked into the meat.

3 Heat the remaining 2 tablespoons of oil in a wok or deep frying pan. Add the chicken to the hot oil and cook for 10–12 minutes, tossing the meat occasionally. Serve hot, arranged with the salad.

OKRA WITH GREEN MANGO AND LENTILS

I f you like okra or "lady's fingers" you'll love this spicy, tangy dish from Pakistan.

INGREDIENTS

115g/4oz/⅔ cup yellow
lentils (toor dhal)
45ml/3 tbsp corn oil
2.5ml/½ tsp onion seeds
2 medium onions, sliced
2.5ml/½ tsp ground fenugreek
5ml/1 tsp ginger pulp
5ml/1 tsp garlic pulp
7.5ml/1½ tsp chilli powder
1.5ml/¼ tsp turmeric
5ml/1 tsp ground coriander
1 green (unripe) mango, peeled
and sliced
450g/1lb okra, cut into 1cm/½in pieces
7.5ml/1½ tsp salt
2 fresh red chillies, seeded and sliced
2 tbsp chopped fresh coriander
1 tomato, sliced

SERVES 4

1 Wash the lentils thoroughly under cold running water, and put in a saucepan with enough water to cover. Bring to the boil and cook until soft but not mushy, for about 30 minutes. Drain thoroughly and set to one side.

2 Heat the oil in a wok and fry the onion seeds until they begin to pop. Add the onions and fry until golden brown. Lower the heat and add the fenugreek, ginger, garlic, chilli powder, turmeric and coriander.

3 Throw in the mango slices and the okra. Stir well and add the salt, red chillies and coriander. Stir-fry for about 3 minutes or until the okra is cooked through.

4 Finally, add the cooked lentils and sliced tomato, combine well, and cook for a further 3 minutes. Serve hot.

BALTI BABY VEGETABLES

There is a wide selection of baby vegetables available, and this simple recipe does full justice to their delicate flavour and attractive appearance. Serve as part of a main meal or a light appetizer.

INGREDIENTS
10 new potatoes, halved
12–14 baby carrots
12–14 baby courgettes
30ml/2 tbsp corn oil
15 baby onions
30ml/2 tbsp chilli sauce
5ml/1 tsp garlic pulp
5ml/1 tsp ginger pulp
5ml/1 tsp salt
400g/14oz/2 cups canned
chick-peas, drained
10 cherry tomatoes
5ml/1 tsp crushed dried red chillies and
30ml/2 tbsp sesame seeds, to garnish

SERVES 4 – 6

1 Bring a medium pan of salted water to the boil and add the potatoes and carrots. After about 12–15 minutes, add the courgettes and boil for a further 5 minutes or until all the vegetables are just tender.

2 Drain the vegetables thoroughly and set to one side.

3 Heat the oil in a deep, round-bottomed frying pan or wok and add the baby onions. Fry until the onions turn golden brown. Lower the heat and add the chilli sauce, garlic, ginger and salt, taking care not to burn the mixture.

4 Add the chick-peas and stir-fry over a medium heat until all the moisture has been absorbed.

5 Add the cooked vegetables and cherry tomatoes and stir with a slotted spoon for about 2 minutes.

6 Garnish with the crushed red chillies and sprinkle with the sesame seeds. Serve immediately.

COOK'S TIP
Try other vegetable combinations, such as baby sweetcorn, French beans, mangetouts, okra and cauliflower or broccoli florets.

PAK CHOI AND MUSHROOM STIR-FRY

T he wild oyster and shiitake mushrooms in this dish have a particularly distinctive, delicate flavour; other types of mushrooms can be used if you can't get hold of these varieties.

INGREDIENTS
4 dried black Chinese mushrooms
450g/1lb pak choi
50g/2oz/¹⁄₄ cup oyster mushrooms
50g/2oz/¹⁄₄ cup shiitake mushrooms
30ml/1 tbsp vegetable oil
1 clove garlic, crushed
30ml/1 tbsp oyster sauce

SERVES 4

2 Tear the pak choi into small pieces with your fingers. Halve the large oyster and shiitake mushrooms, using a sharp knife.

3 Strain the black mushrooms and leave to dry on kitchen paper. Heat the wok or large frying pan, then add the oil. When the oil is hot, stir-fry the garlic until softened but not coloured.

4 Add the pak choi and stir-fry for 1 minute. Mix in all the mushrooms and stir-fry for 1 minute.

1 To soften the black mushrooms, soak in 150ml/¹⁄₄ pint/²⁄₃ cup boiling water for 15 minutes.

5 Add the oyster sauce, coating the mushrooms and pak choi evenly, and serve immediately.

BEAN CURD STIR-FRY

Bean curd has a pleasant creamy texture, which makes a good contrast with crunchy stir-fried vegetables. It is favoured by vegetarians as it is an excellent meat substitute, high in protein and low in fat. Make sure you buy firm bean curd, which cuts easily.

INGREDIENTS
115g/4oz hard white cabbage
2 green chillies
225g/8oz firm bean curd
45ml/3 tbsp vegetable oil
2 cloves garlic, crushed
3 spring onions, chopped
175g/6oz French beans, topped and tailed
175g/6oz baby sweetcorn, halved
115g/4oz beansprouts
45ml/3 tbsp smooth peanut butter
25ml/1½ tbsp dark soy sauce
300ml/½ pint/1¼ cups coconut milk

SERVES 2 – 4

1 Shred the white cabbage thinly and set aside. Carefully remove the seeds from the chillies, chop the flesh finely and set aside. Cut the bean curd into thin strips about 1cm/½in thick.

2 Heat the wok, then add 30ml/2 tbsp of the oil. When the oil is hot, add the bean curd, stir-fry for 3 minutes and remove. Set aside. Wipe out the wok with kitchen paper.

3 Add the remaining oil. When it is hot, add the garlic, cabbage, spring onions and chillies and stir-fry for 1 minute. Add the French beans, sweetcorn and beansprouts and stir-fry for a further 2 minutes.

4 Add the peanut butter and soy sauce. Stir well to coat the vegetables. Add the bean curd to the vegetables.

5 Pour the coconut milk over the vegetables, simmer for 3 minutes and serve immediately.

MANGO ICE CREAM

Mangoes are used widely in Asian cooking, particularly in Thailand, where this deliciously rich ice cream originates.

INGREDIENTS
2 x 425g/15oz cans mango,
sliced and drained
50g/2oz/4 tbsp caster sugar
juice of 1 lime
15ml/1 tbsp powdered gelatine
350ml/12fl oz/1½ cups double cream,
lightly whipped
fresh mint sprigs, to decorate

SERVES 4 – 6

COOK'S TIP
Other fruits can be used in this recipe to make flavoursome ice creams. If you are looking for a dessert to serve after a spicy main course, choose sharp, tangy citrus fruits such as orange, lemon or grapefruit, which will cleanse and refresh the palate and aid digestion.

1 Reserve 4–6 slices of mango for decoration and chop the remainder into small cubes. Place in a bowl with the sugar. Add the lime juice to the mixture.

2 Put 45ml/3 tbsp hot water in a small bowl and sprinkle over the gelatine. Place over a pan of gently simmering water and stir until dissolved. Pour on to the cubed mango and mix well.

3 Add the lightly whipped cream and fold into the mango mixture. Pour the mixture into a polythene freezer bag or box and freeze until half frozen.

4 Place in a food processor or blender and blend until smooth. Spoon back into the polythene bag and refreeze.

5 Remove from the freezer 10 minutes before serving and place in the refrigerator. Serve scoops of the ice cream decorated with pieces of the reserved sliced mango, topped with sprigs of fresh mint.

COCONUT CUSTARD

This traditional dish from Thailand can be baked or steamed and is often served with a selection of fruit such as mango or tamarillo.

INGREDIENTS

4 eggs
75g/3oz/½ cup soft light brown sugar
250ml/8fl oz/1 cup coconut milk
5ml/1 tsp vanilla, rose or jasmine essence
mint leaves and icing sugar, to decorate
fruit slices, to serve

SERVES 4 – 6

1 Preheat the oven to 150°C/300°F/Gas 2. Whisk the eggs and sugar in a bowl until smooth. Add the coconut milk and the essence and blend well together.

2 Strain the mixture and pour into individual ramekins.

3 Stand the ramekins in a roasting pan. Carefully fill the roasting pan with hot water to reach halfway up the outside of the ramekins.

4 Bake for about 35–40 minutes or until the custards are set. (See Cook's Tip.)

5 Remove from the oven and leave to cool. Turn out on to a plate, and serve with sliced fruit. Decorate with mint leaves and a sprinkling of icing sugar.

COOK'S TIP
To test whether custards are set, insert a fine skewer or cocktail stick into the centre of the ramekin. If it comes out clean, they are properly cooked and ready to remove from the oven.

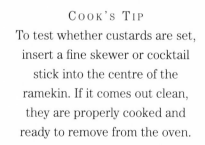

FRIED BANANAS

These treats are popular in Indonesia, where they are often sold in bustling street markets.

INGREDIENTS
115g/4oz/1 cup plain flour
2.5ml/½ tsp bicarbonate of soda
pinch of salt
30ml/2 tbsp granulated sugar
1 egg
90ml/6 tbsp water
30ml/2 tbsp shredded coconut
or 15ml/1 tbsp sesame seeds
4 firm bananas
oil for frying
sugar and 1 lime, cut into wedges,
to serve

SERVES 4

COOK'S TIP
Other fruits such as pineapple, apple and pear can be fried in the same way.

1 Sift the flour, bicarbonate of soda and salt into a bowl. Stir in the granulated sugar. Mix well, then whisk in the egg and add enough water to make a thin batter. Whisk in the coconut or sesame seeds.

2 Peel the bananas and cut each one in half lengthways.

3 Heat the oil in a wok or deep frying pan. Dip the bananas in the batter, then gently drop a few into the oil. Fry until golden brown.

4 Remove from the oil and drain on kitchen paper. Sprinkle with sugar and decorate with the lime wedges. Serve immediately.

LASSI

Lassi is a very popular drink both in India and Pakistan. It is available from both roadside cafes and good hotels. There is no substitute for this drink, especially on a hot day. It is ideal served with hot dishes, as it helps the body to digest spicy food.

INGREDIENTS
300ml/½ pint/1¼ cups natural yogurt
5ml/1 tsp sugar or to taste
300ml/½ pint/1¼ cups iced water
30ml/2 tbsp puréed fruit (optional)
15ml/1 tbsp crushed pistachio nuts

SERVES 4

COOK'S TIP
Fruit purée provides a filling, refreshing addition to traditional lassi. Try using strawberries, raspberries, mangoes and oranges – either fresh or frozen.

1 Place the yogurt in a jug and whisk it for about 2 minutes until frothy. Add the sugar to taste.

2 Pour in the water and the puréed fruit, if using, and continue to whisk for about 2 minutes.

3 Pour the lassi into tall serving glasses. Serve chilled, decorated with crushed pistachio nuts.

HOT TOMATO SAMBAL

S ambals are placed on the table as a condiment and are used mainly for dipping meat and fish. They are quite strong and should be used sparingly.

INGREDIENTS
3 ripe tomatoes
2.5ml/½ tsp salt
5ml/1 tsp chilli sauce
60ml/4 tbsp fish sauce or soy sauce
15ml/1 tbsp chopped coriander leaves

MAKES 120ML/4FL OZ/½ CUP

COOK'S TIP
Hot Tomato Sambal is often used in place of fresh red chillies in many sauces or curries. It can be stored in the refrigerator for up to a week.

1 Cover the tomatoes with boiling water to loosen the skins. Remove the skins, halve, discard the seeds and chop finely.

2 Place the tomatoes in a bowl, add the salt, chilli sauce and fish sauce or soy sauce. Sprinkle with coriander and serve.

SAMBAL GORENG

his sambal makes an excellent, if fiery, side dip for vegetable, fish or meat dishes.

INGREDIENTS

2.5cm/1in cube terasi
2 onions, quartered
2 garlic cloves, crushed
2.5cm/1in lengkuas, peeled and sliced
10ml/2 tsp chilli sambal paste or 2 fresh
red chillies, seeded and sliced
30ml/2 tbsp oil
45ml/3 tbsp tomato purée
600ml/1 pint/2½ cups stock or water
350g/12oz cooked chicken pieces
50g/2oz/⅓ cup cooked French beans
60ml/4 tbsp tamarind juice
pinch of sugar
45ml/3 tbsp coconut milk or cream
salt and freshly ground black pepper

MAKES 900ML/1½ PINTS/3¾ CUPS

COOK'S TIP
For Prawn Sambal Goreng, add
350g/12oz cooked prawns and 1 green
pepper, seeded and chopped. For an
egg version, add 3 hard-boiled eggs,
shelled and chopped, and 2 tomatoes,
skinned, seeded and chopped.

1 Process the *terasi* with the onions and garlic to a paste in a food processor or with a pestle and mortar. Add the *lengkuas*, chilli sambal paste or sliced chillies and salt. Process or pound to a fine paste.

2 Fry the paste in hot oil for 1–2 minutes, without browning, until the mixture gives off a rich aroma.

3 Add the tomato purée and the stock or water and cook over a medium heat for 10 minutes. Add the chicken and French beans (or see Cook's Tip for alternatives) and cook for 3–4 minutes. Stir in the tamarind juice, sugar and coconut milk or cream at the last minute. Season with salt and freshly ground black pepper and serve immediately in small dipping bowls.

HOT LIME PICKLE

A good lime pickle is delicious served with any meal. In India, where it originates, it is thought to increase the appetite and help digestion. It takes a long time to prepare, but is worth the wait!

INGREDIENTS
25 limes
225g/8oz/1 cup salt
50g/2oz/¼ cup fenugreek powder
50g/2oz/¼ cup mustard powder
150g/5oz/½ cup chilli powder
15g/½oz turmeric
600ml/1 pint/2½ cups mustard oil
5ml/1 tsp asafoetida
25g/1oz yellow mustard seeds, crushed

MAKES 450G/1LB/2 CUPS

1 Cut each lime into 8 pieces and remove the pips. Place the limes in a large sterilized jar or glass bowl. Add the salt and toss with the limes. Cover and leave in a warm place until they become soft and brown in colour, for about 1–2 weeks.

2 Mix together the fenugreek powder, mustard powder, chilli powder and turmeric and add to the limes. Cover with a clean cloth and leave to rest in a warm place for a further 2–3 days.

3 Heat the mustard oil in a frying pan and fry the asafoetida and mustard seeds. When the oil reaches smoking point, pour over the limes. Mix well, cover and leave in a warm place for 1 week before serving.

THAI DIPPING SAUCE

N am Prik is the most common dipping sauce in Thailand. It has a fiery strength, so use with caution.

INGREDIENTS
15ml/1 tbsp vegetable oil
1 piece shrimp paste, 1cm/½ in square,
or 15ml/1 tbsp fish sauce
2 cloves garlic, finely sliced
1 piece fresh ginger, 2cm/¾ in long,
peeled and finely chopped
3 small red chillies, seeded and chopped
15ml/1 tbsp finely chopped
coriander root or stem
20ml/4 tsp sugar
45ml/3 tbsp dark soy sauce
juice of ½ lime

MAKES 120ML/4FL OZ/½ CUP

COOK'S TIP
Nam Prik sauce will keep in a screw-top jar for up to 10 days or up to 2 weeks if stored in the refrigerator. As it is such a versatile sauce, suited to many Asian dishes, it's a good idea to make a large quantity as it can be frozen for up to 2 months.

1 Heat the vegetable oil in a wok, add the shrimp paste or fish sauce, garlic, ginger and chillies and soften without colouring, for about 1–2 minutes.

2 Remove from the heat and add the coriander, sugar, soy sauce and lime juice. Serve in a small bowl.

INDEX